Introduction

I have been teaching English as a second language for two decades. My job is, for the most part, to encourage students to speak. My specialty are conversation classes. I wrote this book because there aren't very many books that English teachers can use specifically for conversation classes. There is a lot of material online, it is true. But sometimes you want something quick that you can just take off of your shelf and photocopy. This book should also be useful because it is not connected to one particular time, the subjects are those which students deal with on a daily basis. I wrote something that I wished existed. I hope other English teachers will find it helpful as well.

I have been testing the material for the past few months and I can say that it could be used for students from pre-intermediate to advanced levels. You just have to choose what works with your group and their level. These lessons are designed for an hour, but I never have enough time to do everything. The material could be used as it is, or parts of the lessons could be used as supplemental material. I created the strange facts section just by using Google. Some information may be inaccurate, but that is also a way you can encourage your students to speak, by discussing the truth of these statements. I teach mostly adults, so some material might not be ideal for younger students. You, as a teacher, need to select what is good for them.

That's all from me. Have fun,
    Adam Leverton.

Adventure

"Life is either a great adventure, or it is nothing."

-Helen Keller

Risky venture/a dangerous undertaking/off the beaten track/bucket list/extreme sports/ jeopardize/venture/embark/hazard/thrill

Student A

What has been the biggest adventure of your life?
How do you define adventure, in other words, what does adventure mean for you?
What kind of people have more adventures?
Who is the most adventurous person you know? Why?
On a scale of one to ten, one being you are as adventurous as a turtle, and 10 being you are as adventurous as Indiana Jones, how adventurous are you?

Student B

How can a person make their daily life adventurous?
Choose one: a life full of adventure, a quiet life full of love, a boring life full of money. Why did you make that choice?
Have you had an adventure that has changed your life? Please describe it if you have had such an adventure, and if you haven't, describe an adventure you'd like to have.
What do you think people learn from their adventures?

Debate: Which is better: Travel or Education?

    Travel   Education

Ethics in Adventure

- A child asks you, a rich traveler, for money in a very poor country. What do you do?
- You go to take a picture of a person, who for you, is 'exotic', they ask you for money for the picture. What do you do?
- Many countries repress their citizens. Would you travel there? Why? Why not?
- You are invited to take a tour of a slum. Would you go? Why? Why not?

Ranking

Which are the best and worst places to go on an adventure?

jungle/desert/mountains/sea/space/city

Adventure Program

A television program has randomly selected you to go on an adventure to the Amazon. You have five minutes to pack five things, what do you take?

Film

"A good film is when the price of the dinner, the theater admission and the babysitter were worth it."

-Alfred Hitchcock.

genre/adaptation/special effects/main character/cast/soundtrack/location/thriller/horror/western/romcom

Student A

Tell me about a film that you really enjoyed. Why did you enjoy it so much?
Tell me about a film that you really hated. Why did you hate it so much?
Is there a film that you have seen more than once? Which one and why have you seen it so many times?
What is the scariest film you have ever seen?
What was the first film you went to see in the theater, or one of the first you saw?

Student B

What was the last film you saw? What was it about?
What do you think is the best film from your country?
If your life was made into a film, what genre of film would it be?
If you could live in the world of any film, what film would you live in? Why?
Where do you prefer to watch movies? Why?

Debate:

<u>Watching films at home</u>   <u>Watching films at the cinema</u>

Movie Guessing

Describe the plot (story) of a famous movie to your partner, they have to guess which movie it is.

Movie Role Play

Your teacher will give you a partner, and tell you both the name of a film you will act out in front of the class.

Movie Quotes

Guess the movies these famous quotes come from:

Frankly, my dear, I don't give a damn.

I'm gonna make him an offer he can't refuse.

You don't understand! I coulda had class. I coulda been a contender. I could've been somebody, instead of a bum, which is what I am.

Toto, I've a feeling we're not in Kansas anymore.

Here's looking at you, kid.

Go ahead, make my day.

All right, Mr. DeMille, I'm ready for my close-up.

May the Force be with you.

Music

"Without music, life would be a mistake."

-Friedrich Nietzsche

acoustic/bass/amplify/chorus/bar/catchy/duo/explicit/genre/harmony/groove

Student A

What kind of music do you enjoy?

What kind of music do you hate?

Do you play any instrument? If you don't, if you could, what instrument would you like to learn how to play?

Imagine your neighbor's child started to learn an instrument. Which would be the worst for you to listen to her practice?

Is there is any song that has special memories for you? What is it?

Student B

Do you pay more attention to the lyrics or to the music when you listen to music?

Where and when do you listen to music? How much music do you listen to every week?

Name five genres of music and tell me what you think about them, and how they are different from other kinds of genres.

When was the last concert you went to see? Who did you see?

If you could go to any concert, which singer or group's concert would you want to see? Why?

Debate: Everyone should learn a musical instrument

For   Against

Song line conversation

With your partner you can have a conversation using only lyrics from a song.

Find someone who….

Likes the same music as you do. Hates the same music as you do.

Party

You can invite any musician, or musical group to your birthday party, living or dead. You and your partner must agree on the person.

Strange Music Facts

- Guitar strings were originally made from sheep intestines.
- Monaco's orchestra is bigger than its army.
- The Beatles' drummer, Ringo Starr appeared in a Japanese commercial for apple sauce, because 'ringo' means apple in Japanese.
- Hayden's skull was removed from its grave. A 'replacement' was found and then the original was found. Both remain in the grave.
- In the opera, Don Giovanni boasts that he seduced 1001 Spanish, 640 Italian, 231 German, 100 French and 91 Turkish women.

Neighbors

"You can change friends, but not neighbors."

-Atal Bihari Vajpayee

Next door/neighborhood/neighborly/good fences make good neighbors/

Student A

What does it mean to be a good neighbor?
Who is the best neighbor you've had?
Who is the worst neighbor you've had?
Tell me about a time when you were a bad neighbor?
Tell me about a time when you were a good neighbor?

Student B

How well do you know your neighbors? Would you like to know them better or worse?
If you could have anyone live next door to you, who would you want to live next door?
What kind of neighbor are you?
How do you react when you have problems with your neighbors?
How do you react when your neighbors have problems with you?

Debate: Neighbors have a duty to inform the police of any suspicious behavior they see

For   Against

Ranking: Which neighbor would be the worst? Which would be the best?

An elderly couple/three young university students/a young family/a single bachelor/a very large family/a person with a lot of dogs/a person with a lot of exotic pets/a smoker

Role-play:

Student A: Your neighbor is always having loud parties and you have to get up early most days for work. Try to resolve the situation.

Student B: Your neighbor is always complaining about your partying, but you moved into the neighborhood because of its great nightlife. Try to resolve the situation.

The Worst Neighbors Ever

- Phillip Roger Bennett tried to burn down his neighbor's, house because the grass was too long. The neighbor's daughter was inside the house at the time.
- Jeffrey Wright hired a hit man to kill a neighbor because of argument about where cars should be parked.
- David Constantine was banned from his own home after constantly harassing his neighbors.
- Anthony James David took his neighbors out to an NFL game, he paid for it with the credit card he had stolen from his neighbor.
- A neighbor won the lottery and built a 24-hour race track in a wealthy neighborhood.

Money

-Kinky Friedman

currency/bankrupt/account/cashier/debit/credit card/debt/mortgage/owe/bargain

Student A

How much money, for you, is too much?
How much money, for you, is too little?
Can you think of a time when money made you happy? Tell me.
Can you think of a time when money made you unhappy? Tell me.
How much money would you like to have in your bank account right now?

Student B

What is the secret to making a fortune?
What did your parents teach you about money?
What do you wish you knew about money? How would that change your life?
If you had a large amount of money, how would your life change?
What's better, to be famous or to be rich? Why?

Debate: Money is the root of all evil

<u>For</u>   <u>Against</u>

1 Billion dollars

You and your partner have won a million dollars. Together, decide what you are going to do with it.

Ranking

Which of these people would you give 30, 000 dollars to? Decide with your partner.

A single mother/a single father/your friend/your mom or dad/a person with a great business idea/a homeless person

Strange Money Facts

- There are more credit cards than people in the U.S.
- In the U.S., more Monopoly money is printed than real money every year.
- If you have 10$ in your pocket and no debt, you are more wealthy than 25% of Americans.
- The International Space Station is the most expensive object ever built-$150 Billion.
- Pablo Escobar, illegal drug entrepreneur, had so much money that at one point rats were eating $1 billion in cash of his money every year.

Lies

"I love you and because I love you I would sooner have you hate me for telling you the truth than adore me for telling you lies."

-Pietro Aretino

Bald faced lie/white lie/live a lie/lie through one's teeth/put the lie to something/false pretenses/a tall tale/bend the truth/economical with the truth/pack of lies

Student A

What is the biggest lie you have ever told to someone?
What is the biggest lie someone has ever told to you?
Who do you think lies the most, men or women? Why?
What profession, apart from politicians, lies the most?
Are lies sometimes necessary? When?

Student B

Are you a good liar? Why? Why not?
Think about a situation where you don't directly lie, but you are not honest with another person.
For example, you are having an affair with your partner's sister. Are you lying? Why? Why not?
What's the difference between a lie and an exaggeration?
Everyone says they want people to be honest with them. Is that really true? Why do you think so?

Game: 1 Lie and 2 Truths

Tell your partner two things about you that are true, and one thing which is false. Your partner has to guess which are true and which is false.

The Worst

Rank these situations. When is the worst time to lie?

On a first date/during a job interview/during a wedding ceremony/during a funeral/at the doctor's

OK to lie

In which situations is it okay (for you) to lie

A surprise birthday/a very sick child's parents have died/your father has dementia, he wants to see his wife who has passed away/a family member asks a doctor if a relative (husband, wife, child, parent) died a painful death/a scientist gives a test subject a placebo to test a real treatment/a politician lies to the public to keep his country safe/a woman is asked during a job interview if she intends to start a family/your child starts to be interested in something creative, like singing, but they are not good (yet)/during a business negotiation

Language

> "The limits of my language means the limits of my world."

-Ludwig Wittgenstein

Body languages/loaded language/in plain language/language that would fry bacon/speak the same language/foul language/beyond words/talk is cheap/words fail me/it's all Greek to me

Student A

What do you like about your native language?
What do you dislike about your native language?
What do you like about English?
What do you dislike about English?
What do you think is the easiest language to learn? Which is the hardest?

Student B

How many languages do you speak? Which ones?
How many languages would you like to speak? Which ones?
How was the language education you received in your school? What was good and what could be improved?
Please tell me your opinion about three different languages.
Tell me about a time when you spoke a different language with a foreigner.

Debate: All school subjects in your country should be taught in English

<u>For</u>   <u>Against</u>

Ranking:

Discuss with your partner how you feel about the following languages:

french/spanish/english/german/japanese/chinese/arabic

Borrowed Words

With your partner, try to find five words in English borrowed from another language.

Strange English Facts

- 'Go!' is the shortest sentence in English.
- Pneumonoultramicroscopicsilicovolcanoconiosis is the longest word in English. It's a disease caused by inhaling ash and dust.
- I/we/two/three are the oldest words in the English language.
- Girl used to mean small boy or girl.
- The word 'set' has the most meanings.

Jokes and Humor

"Life is hard. It is not too short, it is too long. But you have to learn how to live; you have to have a sense of humour.

-Carolina Herrera

wit/satire/jest/gallows humor/gag/dry humor/amusing/crack up/I don't get it/laughingstock

Student A

Who is the funniest person you know?
When was the last time you had a laughing fit?
What is the funniest film you have watched?
Try to tell me a joke in English.
What things or situations do you find funny?

Student B

What sort of things would you never laugh at?
Tell me about a time when everyone laughed at you?
Have you ever been offended by a joke someone told you? What happened?
Tell me about something you think is a joke, something that should be better than it is.
Why do you think your choice is a joke?
Has someone ever played a joke on you? What happened?

Debate: Is it ever okay to make fun of someone because of their religion, gender, race, etc.

For   Against

Read these jokes with a partner. Which do you find funny?

A woman gets on a bus with her baby. The driver says: 'Ugh, that's the ugliest baby I've ever seen!" The woman walks to the rear of the bus and sits down, fuming. She says to the man next to her: "The driver just insulted me!" The man says: "You go up there and tell him off. Go on, I'll hold your monkey for you."

I went to the zoo the other day. There was only a dog in it - it was a shih tzu.

"I said to the gym teacher: 'Can you teach me to do the splits?' He said: 'How flexible are you?' I said: 'I can't make Tuesdays.'"

Police arrested two kids yesterday, one was drinking battery acid, the other was eating fireworks. They charged one - and let the other off.

"Doc, I can't stop singing The Green, Green Grass of Home. He said: 'That sounds like Tom Jones syndrome.' 'Is it common?' I asked. 'It's not unusual' he replied.

I'm on a whiskey diet. I've lost three days already.

A man walks into a bar with a roll of Tarmac under his arm and says: "Pint please... and one for the road."

I went to the doctor the other day and said: "Have you got anything for wind?" So he gave me a kite.

My mother-in-law fell down a wishing well. I was amazed, I never knew they worked.

Two fish in a tank. One says: "How do you drive this thing?"

I went to buy some camouflage trousers the other day - but I couldn't find any.

When Susan's boyfriend proposed she said: "I love the simple things in life, but I don't want one of them as a husband".

My therapist says I have a preoccupation with vengeance. We'll see about that.

Insects

-Andrea Arnold

fleas/ants/bees/beetles/bugs/fumigation/pest/larvae/ladybug/ladybird/maggots

Student A

Tell me a few ways that insects help people.
Many people are disgusted by insects. Why is this?
What kind of insects can be found in your country?
Have you had any negative experiences, or positive experiences connected to insects? Tell me about them.
What do you think is the scariest insect? Why?

Student B

What do you think is the friendliest insect? Why?
If you could be any insect for an hour, which would you choose? Why?
Do any insects live in your house or apartment? Which ones?
What have you done to try to stop them?
What do you think insects think of us?
What do you think about eating insects? Why?

Debate: We need to protect insects from extinction

For   **Against**

Find some who….

Is afraid of insects/who has had a cockroach in their flat, room or hotel room/has killed an insect recently/was bitten by an insect last year

Alphabet

In the class, the teacher chooses a student randomly, and then that student has to say the name of an insect that starts with a, then the next student with b, until a person can't think of an insect name.

Strange Insect Facts

- Beetles are the most diverse group of creatures known-with over 380, 000 species.
- There are 1.4 million ants per human alive on the planet. That's a lot of ants.
- Insects live on every continent, yes, even Antarctica, but not in the ocean.
- Insect don't have lungs, and breathe through their sides.
- They were the first animals to live on land.
- The biggest insect to ever live was a dragonfly with a wingspan of almost one meter.
- Termite queens can live for fifty years.
- Some honeybee queens quack.
- A caterpillar has more muscles than a human.
- Some ants can explode when they are attacked.

Work

"Success is no accident. It is hard work, perseverance, learning, studying, sacrifice and most of all, love of what you are doing or learning to do."

-Pele

quit/retire/to be laid off/to be fired/raise/hire/commute/shift/part-time/full-time

Student A

If you could work anywhere, where would you work? Why?
Where would you never work? Why?
Why do you work where you work?
If you are not working, why do you want to work where you want to work?
What is the best thing about working?
What is the worst thing about working?

Student B

What is the easiest job, in your opinion?
What is the hardest job, in your opinion?
What did you want to do when you grew up?
Would you prefer to do many different jobs in your life, or would you prefer to stick with one career?
What would you like to do when you retire?

Debate: Working during high school helps students learn responsibility

<u>For</u>   <u>Against</u>

Ranking: Which of these are the best jobs? Which are the worst?

plumber/stockbroker/accountant/sales representative/writer/singer/actor/

Interview:

Pretend that your partner is applying for your job. Interview him or her.

Strange Work Facts

- Monday is the most common sick day, except for Australia where it's Tuesday.
- Friday is the least common sick day.
- People who work full time from 20-65, will have worked 90, 000 hours.
- The most common job in North America is retail.
- In Germany, women must wear a bra to work.
- The Netherlands has the shortest work week, at 29 hours.
- 10, 000 workers die per year of exhaustion in Japan.
- 46% of people fail in their new job, because of an inability to adjust to a new work culture.
- 71% of American workers don't care about their job.
- Americans spend 100 hours per year on average commuting.

History

> "We are not makers of history. We are made by history."

-Martin Luther, Jr.

diplomacy/curtail/ally/arsenal/fiasco/furor/cede/devastate/dissenter/colonize/

Student A

What period of history is the most interesting for you?
What from our time, do you think history will remember?
How could history be taught to children better?
If you could speak to anyone from history, who would you speak to and what would you ask?
Do you think people as a species and as individuals will ever learn from their mistakes? Why or why not?
Can you think of a time when you learned from your mistakes? What happened?

Student B

How do you think our time is different from the past?
How do you think our time is similar to the past?
What historical event has had the biggest impact of your life? Why?
Can you think of something that used to be a problem in the past, that is no longer a problem now?
Imagine you wake up 100 years ago. How is life different?
Imagine you wake up 1000 years ago. How is life different?

Debate: People should have a good understanding of the history of the world

<u>For</u>   <u>Against</u>

20 questions:

Think of a historical person. Your partner has twenty yes or no questions to find out who it is.

Interview:

The teacher will choose a student. The class will choose a famous person. That student will pretend to be the historical figure. Each student has to ask the historical person a question.

Strange History Facts

- The longest war in history was between the Netherlands and the Isles of Scilly, which lasted from 1651 to 1986. There were no casualties.
- The Anglo-Zanzibar war lasted 38 minutes.
- Albert Einstein was offered the presidency of Israel in 1952, but declined the honor.
- Napoleon was once attacked by a bunch of rabbits.
- A Paris orphanage held a fundraiser-the prizes were human babies.
- A man from New Orleans once hired a pirate in an attempt to rescue Napoleon.
- Arabic numbers were invented by Indians.
- Iceland's parliament is the oldest in the world-it was established in 930.
- Egyptians used stones as pillows.

Hair

Hair salon/barbershop/barber/hairdresser/trim/dye/bangs/buzz cut/split ends/highlights

Student A

Do you like your hair? Why or why not?
What is the craziest hair style you've had?
What is the craziest hairstyle you've seen?
What do you do to keep your hair clean and healthy?
How often do you go to the hairdressers?

Student B

If you do go to the hairdressers, do you have one that you always go to, or do you just go to whoever is available?
If you do go to the hairdressers, how much do you spend?
Do you think that is cheap or expensive?
Do you think we should accept the signs of aging, like grey hair, and going bald, or should we try to hide them? Why?
Who has the best hair of anyone you know? What does it look like?
In a perfect world, what would your hair look like?

Debate: You can tell a lot about a person's character by their hair

For	Against

Role-play:

Your partner is your hairdresser. Ask him/her for a new hairstyle and get some advice. When you have finished switch roles.

Best/worst

Tell your partner what you think is the best hairstyle is, and what you think is the worst hairstyle.

Strange Hair Facts

- Hair is made of keratin, the same substance that beaks, feathers, nails and hoofs are made of.
- Your hair can expand by 30% when wet.
- Hair grows faster during warmer weather.
- Your hair is dead, except where it is connected to your head.
- Men's hair and women's hair are physically the same.
- Black hair is the most common in the world, and red is the rarest.
- Blondes have the most strands of hair, redheads the fewest.
- A strand of hair can last five years.
- 80% of Americans wash their hair twice a day.
- You lose 40-150 strands of hair a day, unless you are bald.

Hate

"It is easy to hate and difficult to love. This is how the whole scheme of things works. All good things are difficult to achieve; and bad things are very easy to get."

-Confucius

To hate someone's guts/pet hate/love-hate relationship/can't stomach something/aversion/gripe/loathing/nuisance/revulsion

Student A

What kinds of things do you hate?
What kinds of people do you hate?
What kinds of food do you hate?
What kinds of music do you have?
What kinds of films and television do you hate?

Student B

Is there anything that you used to hate, but not now? Why?
Do you think it is easy to hate something or hard?
Is it possible for people to learn not to hate each other? Why or why not?
Is there any cure for hatred? If there is, what do you think it is?
Is it ever ok to hate someone? When and why?

Debate: Hatred is natural

For   Against

I hate to bother you….

Please get your partner to stop doing the following things by saying the following things:

smoking/talking too loud on the phone/stinky food/dog has poohed in your yard

Pet Hates…

Write down four of your pet hates. Explain to your partner why you hate them.

Strange Facts about Hate

- People who post many pictures on Facebook, are less likely to have friends.
- People believe that atheists would be less likely to leave a note after damaging someone's car.
- People find people with wide faces untrustworthy.
- When asked to draw a criminal, 82% of people drew a man with facial hair.
- If you pay someone a compliment, others who hear it may become jealous.
- There are two types of sweat. Exercise sweat and stress sweat. People tend to hate people who stress sweat.
- Studies have shown that people tend to think about people who are passionate about something in stereotypes.
- A study was done and respondents claimed that women who enjoyed chemistry were 'maladjusted'.
- Another study discovered that male self-esteem suffered when their female partners were successful.
- Your loneliness can be contagious.

Government and Politics

-Victor Pinchuk

president/prime minister/dictator/legislator/mayor/citizen/debate/campaign/opposition/privilege

Student A

In what areas do you think your government is doing a bad job?
In what areas do you think your government is doing a good job?
What changes in law or policy need to be introduced in your country, in your opinion?
Would you ever consider being a politician? Why or why not?
If you did end up as a politician, how do you think you would be good at it, and how do you think you would be bad at?

Student B

Are people too interested or not enough interested in politics in your country?
Is there any politician you think has done, or is doing a good job? Why?
Describe the best political decision that has recently been made in your country?
What is your opinion of politicians?
Many people say politicians lie all the time. Do you think people really want politicians to be honest?

Debate: Politics is important

For					Against

President….

You are the president of your country. With your partner, discuss how you would solve the following problems:

unemployment/environment problems/crime/corruption

Celebrity leader…

Write down five famous people. Discuss with your partner who you think would be the best leader of the country.

Strange Facts about Politics

- Afghanistanism means to focus on distant parts of the world in order to ignore local issues.
- India is the largest democracy with 700 million voters.
- David "Screaming Lord Sutch", as leader of the Monster Raving Loony Party, was Britain's longest serving party leader until he hung himself in June 1999.
- Although the United States of America was established in 1776 the first American president ever to visit Europe while in office was Woodrow Wilson in 1918.
- Victoria Woodhull (1838-1927) was the first woman to run for office of US President. She and her sister were the first women to run a Wall Street brokerage (1870).
- In 1967, Australia's Prime Minister Harold Holt decided to go for a swim and was never seen again.
- Richard Nixon funded his first political campaign from his winnings in poker.
- Abraham Lincoln was a bartender.

Religion and spirituality

-Swami Vivekananda

agnosticism/ blasphemy/gospel truth/heresy/jihad/crusade/lay/orthodox/secular/pagan

Student A

How would you describe your religious or spiritual views?
What do you think happens after we die?
Are religion and freedom compatible? For example, many religious teach against customs that many consider to be rights, like the right to divorce. Is it possible to have a society where people are religious and free? Why do think so?
A similar question: do you think science and religion are compatible?
What do you appreciate the most about your religion or the religion you grew up in?

Student B

What do you dislike about your religion or the religion you grew up in?
What makes your religion unique in comparison to others?
How is your religion similar to others?
Many people claim that very few people are actually religious but make a show of being religious.
Do you think this is true, or do you think many people are sincere?
If you could ask God one question, what would it be?

Debate: Religion should be a subject which is taught in public schools

    For   Against

Religious knowledge:

Part 1

What do you know about the following religions?

islam/christianity/buddhism/judaism/hinduism/

Part 2

Explain the following celebrations:

christmas/easter/ramadan/passover/diwali/kwanzaa

Strange Facts about Religion

- Oral Roberts, an American televangelist told his viewers that if he didn't get 8 million dollars in three months, he would be killed by god.
- Manhattan is encircled by a string so Orthodox Jews can go outside during the Sabbath.
- France once banned an ad featuring a female Jesus.
- Jehovah's Witnesses believe that Satan and other demons were cast out of heaven on Oct. 1st, 1914.
- Vladimir the Great, the Czar of Russia, decided against converting to Islam because alcohol was banned.
- A man in Taiwan was mauled by lions after an attempt to convert them to Christianity.
- Daniel Everett travelled into the Amazon in the 1970s to convert a tribe to Christianity. They converted him to their religion instead.
- There are 10, 000 religions and 33 830 denominations of Christianity.

Fear

afraid/frightened/scared/feel uneasy/spooked/terrified/petrified/ordeal/shivers/shake

Student A

What is something that scares you?
What is something that used to scare you, but no longer does?
Do know anyone with any strong phobias? What are they scared of?
What is the scariest film you have ever seen?
When were the most scared in your life?

Student B

How do you react when you are afraid?
What is your biggest fear for your future?
Are you scared of fear, or do you like to be thrilled?
Do you know anyone with unusual fears? What are they?
Is fear based on the known, the unknown or both?

Debate: Everyone should face their fears and phobias

For   Against

Fears...

Which of these fears do you share? How did you develop it?

Fear of flying/fear of germs/claustrophobia/fear of storms/fear of dogs/agoraphobia/fear of heights/fear of snakes/fear of spiders

Cure….

How would you cure the above fears? Discuss with your partner.

Strange Facts about Fear

- There are over 400 phobias.
- Americans have a higher chance of dating Taylor Swift, than they do of dying because of Bird Flu.
- The mentally ill are twice as likely to be the victims of violent crime than commit it.
- In 2014, more Americans were killed by toddlers than by terrorists.
- You are more likely to get a computer virus from a church website, than from a porn site.
- More people are killed by vending machines than by sharks.
- Less than 7 people per year are killed by poisonous spiders in the US.
- Deer are the most dangerous wild animal in North America.
- You are six times more likely to be killed by a pig than by a shark.
- Falling coconuts also kill more people per year than sharks.
- 90% of people involved in air crashes, survive.

Advertising

Product placement/jingle/slogan/hype/plug/buzz/endorsements/commercial/classifieds/word of mouth

Student A

What kind of advertising is the most effective for you? Why?

What makes a memorable advertisement?

Tell me about an advertisement you remember and tell me why it was so memorable?

What do you think about advertisers that use controversy to sell their products? Can you give any examples?

Would restrictions on junk food advertising reduce obesity, why or why not?

Student B

Have you tried any product because of word of mouth? Which one?

Give an example of a celebrity endorsement. Did you ever buy that product?

Can you think of time when you noticed product placement in a film or television series? Tell us.

Think of a slogan for yourself.

Can you think of a time when a new film, book, album, game, etc, didn't live up to its hype? Tell us what happened.

Debate: Advertising to children should be banned

For   Against

Sell yourself….

Imagine yourself as a product, try to sell yourself to your partner. Advertise your positive features.

Selling snow to the Inuit

Try to sell the class the following things: dirt/water/air/fire/garbage/time

Strange Facts about Advertising

- $500 billion dollars every year is spent on advertising.
- A 65-year-old American has probably seen two million advertisements per year.
- Billboards were invented in the United States in 1900.
- Most watches in ads are set to 10:10, because the hands on the watch make a happy face.
- US Pharmaceutical companies spend twice as much on advertising as they do on research.

Freedom

"Just living is not enough… one must have sunshine, freedom, and a little flower."

-Hans Christian Anderson

censorship/ban/repression/offensive/liberty/free will/set free/break free/get free/home free

Student A

Please define what freedom means for you.

Do you think your freedom has ever been limited? By what?
In which areas of life do we need more freedom? Why?
In which areas of life do we need less freedom? Why?
When in your life do you feel the freest?

Student B

When in your life have you felt the freest?
Where in the world do you think people are the most free?
Do you think you will have more or less freedom in the future? Why?
Do you think your country will have more or less freedom in the future? Why?
What kind of person is the freest?

Debate: People should have the right to say whatever they want

For   Against

What's the most important freedom for you?

speech/religion/movement/sexuality/belief/from want/from fear

Symbols……

Write down four symbols of freedom. Why did you choose these? Discuss with your partner.

National Days

- France celebrates Bastille Day, July 14th, by host Fireman balls throughout the country. Firefighters host dances and banquets.
- India celebrates its Independence Day on August 15th by flying kites, and sometimes having kite battles.
- South Korea celebrates its freedom on the same day. The president gives pardons to prisoners.
- Indonesia celebrates its freedom a few days later on August 17th by hosting cooking contests, shrimp cookie eating competitions and palm tree climbing.

How does your country celebrate its national day? How do you think it should?

Advice

Grammar note

The word advice is uncountable. I give you some advice. ~~I give you some advices.~~ Advice is a noun. Advise is a verb. I advise you to go to Jessica for some help.

a free bit of advice/dutch uncle/sage advice/encouragement/tip/ guidance/proposal/instruction/consultation/suggestion

Student A

Who has given you the best advice in your life? Who do you turn to for help?
Tell me about a time when you should have taken advice, but didn't. What happened?
Tell me about a time when you should not have taken advice but did. What happened?
What kind of person can give the best advice? Why?
What kind of person can give the worst advice? Why?

Student B

Do you think the advice you give to your family and friends is useful? Why or why not?
If you could ask anyone for advice about any subject, who would you ask, and why?
Is there anyone who you refuse to give advice. Why?
Is there someone who really should listen to your advice? Who?
When have you needed advice the most?

Give the following people advice:

Jessica is a single mother, and she wants to spend more quality time with her young children.
Dwight thinks he has feelings for a good female friend.
Erica has been working at one company for a few years and still hasn't been promoted.
John loves spiders. It's his passion. His girlfriend is arachnophobic.
Terry eats too much. He can't stop. He's tried everything.

Ask your partner for advice about the following situations:

love/work/health/stress/goals/

<u>Helpful expressions:</u>

If I were you…..
If I were in your shoes…
I think you should…
I think you shouldn't….
What you need to do...

Medicine/Health

-Buddha

physician/surgeon/pharmacy/prescription/shot/diagnosis/headache/cast/fracture/exam

Student A

How healthy are you?
What is the most unhealthy thing you do?
What is the most healthy thing you do?
What should you do if you want to be more healthy?
Do you think it is possible to be healthy in modern civilization? Why or why not?

Student B

What do you do to take care of your body?
What do you do to take care of your mind?
Which unhealthy habits have you quit? How long did it take you?
Which healthy habits have you pick up? How long did it take you?
Who is the healthiest person you know? What makes them so healthy?

Debate: All health care should be paid for by the government

For   Against

Cures:

How would you treat the following symptoms? Discuss with your partner:

pain/fatigue/infection/swelling/headache/fever/nausea/itch/allergy/depression

Healthy/Unhealthy

Tell your partner about three healthy things you do, and three healthy things you do.

Strange Facts about Health

- Your feet can get larger with age.
- Women are more prone to feeling cold than men.
- People smell better with age.
- Humans rarely wake up at night to defecate.
- Human sweat only stinks if it comes from the armpits.
- Dogs can smell cancer and low blood sugar.
- You are more likely to have a heart attack on a Monday.

Ambition

"Ambition is the path to success. Persistence is the vehicle you arrive in."

-Bill Bradley

aspire/attain/diligent/objective/pitfall/steadfast/yearning/zeal/surpass/vacillate

Student A

What would you like to achieve in your life?
Tell me about a goal that you achieved?
Who is the most ambitious person you know? What makes them so ambitious?
Tell me about a goal that you failed to achieve?
What do you think is the most dangerous ambition?

Student B

What ambitions did your parent have, or do your parents have for you?
What ambitions do you have for your children, or would you have for your children?
How have your ambitions changed over the years?
Do your family or friends have any unusual ambitions? What are they?
Is it better to have many ambitions or few? Why?

Debate: Successful people are the most ambitious

For   Against

Ranking:

Which people are the most and least ambitious in your opinion? Discuss with a partner.

athlete/politician/artist/musician/entrepreneur/

Ambitions for other people:

What are your ambitions for: your family/your city/your country/your planet discuss with a partner.

Ambitious People

Benjamin Franklin was the 15th of 17 children, and the son of a candle maker. He studied hard and at the age of seventeen moved to Philadelphia where he started his own printing press and became independently wealthy. This gave him the time to become a writer, inventor, and statesman.

Ross Perot was the son of a Texas cotton broker. He joined the U.S. Navy. After he was discharged he got a job as a salesman with IBM. He made the yearly sales quota in a week. He started his own company that was purchased by GM for 100 million. He used the money to get involved in politics, and ran as an independent for president.

John D. Rockefeller was the son of an absent salesman. He worked as a bookkeeper until he invested in an oil well with some friends. He kept investing and consolidating until his business was worth 1.5 billion dollars (in 1937) at the time of his death. He donated most of his personal fortune to charity.

Ralph Lauren was the son of poor Jewish immigrants. He never finished school and never had any training. He got a job in a men's clothing store, and started to design his own ties. He built this business into a world-famous fashion brand.

Anger

"When anger rises, think of the consequences."

-Confucius

See red/irritated/annoyed/grumpy/get up on the wrong side of the bed/pissed off/furious/blow your top/to go ballistic/to be beside yourself

Student A

What things make you angry?
What kind of people make you angry?
Is there anything that used to make you angry that does anymore?
Who is the angriest person you know? Why do you think they are so angry?
Who is the calmest person you know? What do you think makes them so calm?

Student B

How do you show the world that you are angry?
Do you think it is healthier to hide your anger, or to show it to the world?
What is the best way to deal with angry people?
In what situations do you feel comfortable getting angry?
In what situations do you feel uncomfortable getting angry?

Debate: It is better to express our anger than hide it

For   Against

Which of these things make you the most angry, and why?

people who walk slow/stubbing your toe/people who cut in line/when people talk to you when you are talking on the phone/self-checkout machines/someone reading over your shoulder/

Calm down….

Write down five methods for calming down that you use and discuss them with your partner.

Myths about Anger

Discuss these myths about anger, and why you think there are myths. Or maybe you think they are facts.

- Not all anger is destructive.
- Anger is not an all powerful feeling. There are degrees.
- You don't have to 'release' your anger.
- Not all angry people yell and scream.
- Dealing with your anger doesn't mean keeping quiet. It means thinking about what you are doing.

Animals

"An animal's eyes have the power to speak a great language."

-Martin Buber

The elephant in the room/that really gets my goat/the cat's meow/wild goose chase/like a fish out of water/ants in your pants/one trick pony/pig headed/let the cat out of the bag/red herring

Student A

What kind of animals do you have as pets? If you don't have any pets, what pets would you like to have?
What kind of animals live in your city or near your home?
What kinds of animals are mistreated in your country? How are they mistreated?
What kinds of rights do you think animals have?
Tell me about any experiences you have had with wild animals.

Student B

Have you ever been or almost been attacked by an animal? What happened?
If you could be any animal, what animal would you be?
What kind of animals symbolize your country or town? Why were those chosen?
What do you think is the most dangerous animal in the world? Why?
Which is the most useful animal?

Debate: Animals and people are not the same

For   Against

Twenty Questions

Think of an animal. The class has to guess the animal, using only yes/no questions and has only twenty questions to guess.

Animal Role play

Say the name of an animal. Your partner has to think of three ways that animal's life would be similar to their own, and three ways it would be different.

Pet Names

Think of good names for the following pet animals: *a cat, a dog, a turtle, a spider, a frog, a rabbit, a hamster.*

Weird Animal Facts

- Gorillas can catch human infections such as the common cold.
- Ostriches can run faster than horses, and can roar like lions.
- A lion only kills about twenty animals a year, and female lions are responsible for 90% of the kills.
- Almost half of all pigs live in China
- Dogs have better eyesight than humans, just not as colorful.
- Only three mammals have menopause-elephants, humpback whales and humans.
- A tarantula can survive for more than two years without food.
- Alligators can live up to one hundred years.
- A housefly hums in the key of F.
- Ants never sleep.

Beauty

-John Ray

Beauty mark/beauty queen/a thing of beauty is a joy forever/age before beauty/beauty is in the eye of the beholder/beauty is only skin deep/beauty sleep/bevy of beauties/not going to win any beauty contests/that's the beauty of

Student A

How much time every day do you spend on your appearance? Do you think that is enough, not enough or too much?
Who is the most beautiful person you know, and why?
When you meet someone for the first time, what physical thing do you notice first?
When you meet someone for the first time, what do you pay attention to in terms of fashion?
What would make you less beautiful?

Student B

What does your culture find beautiful that others don't?
Do you think plastic surgery is acceptable? Why or why not?
What do you find beautiful that other people don't?
Where is the most beautiful place that you have ever been?
What is the most beautiful thing that a person can do for another person?

Debate: People care too much about how they look

For   Against

All the beautiful people…

Write down five people you think are beautiful. Compare them with a partner. Why did you choose the people on your list?

Neighborhood improvement…

Think of five ways you can make your country, town or community more beautiful. Share them with your partner.

Weird Beauty Facts

- During WWII, nurses always wore lipstick, as a morale boost for injured soldiers.
- The left side of the face is more attractive than the right.
- In the 1930s, many brands of radioactive beauty products were sold.
- Women spend, on average, 58 days of their lives, shaving or waxing hair.
- Fingernails grow faster in the summer, than in the winter, and the nails on your dominant hand also grow faster.
- Women spend thirteen days of their lives applying makeup.
- The average woman buys seven new pairs of shoes a year.
- Women used to shave and pluck the hair on their heads to ensure a high hairline during the Renaissance.
- 60% of twelve year old girls use cosmetics.
- The first nail polish was invented in China in 3000 bc.

Art

"The purpose of art is washing the dust of daily life off our souls."

-Pablo Picasso

Down to a fine art/art is long and life is short/state of the art/work of art/blank canvas/con artist/poetic justice/to paint something with a broad brush/tar with the same brush/flim flam artist

Student A

What kind of art do you enjoy?
What kind of art do you dislike?
In what way are you artistic? Please answer the question, even if you think you are not artistic.
When was the last time you went to an art gallery or a museum?
Who are some famous artists from your country?

Student B

Is there a style of art which is unique to your country or culture? Please describe it.
What was the last piece of art (painting/poster/drawing/picture) that you bought? Describe it and tell me why you bought it?
Describe what kind of artistic decorations you have in your home.
What does art mean for you?
How could art be made to be more popular?

Debate: Art lessons should be a vital part of education

For   Against

Drawing…

The teacher will choose people to come up to the board, and draw a word. The rest of the class has to guess, in English what the student is drawing.

In the painting….

The teacher brings in four famous paintings. The student have to imagine that they are inside the painting.

Weird Artist Facts

- Pablo Picasso carried a gun around with him to threaten people who annoyed him.
- Leonard da Vinci was a vegetarian.
- Michelangelo never bathed.
- Salvador Dali stole pens.
- Andy Warhol made many time capsules.
- Paul Gauguin was a fencer.
- Wassily Kandinsky had synesthesia.
- There are only fifteen paintings left by Leonardo da Vinci.
- Claude Monet's father wanted him to be a grocer.

The esoteric

"From a young age, I was obsessed with the mysterious, the esoteric, the paranormal."

-Drummond Money-Coutts

divination/slight of hand/lore/gut feeling/pseudoscience/fortune telling/prophecy/zodiac/star sign/sign

Student A

Do you believe in the supernatural? Why or why not?

What is your star sign? Do you think it has any influence on your life?

Have you ever been to a fortune teller? Would you ever go? Why or why not?

Have you ever had a mystical experience? Tell us what happened.

What is your explanation of deja vu?

Student B

Have you or anyone else seen a ghost? Please tell us that story if you have. If you haven't what do you think the explanation is for ghost sightings?

What superstitions do you believe in?

Do you believe that your dreams can tell you about your future?

Do you think you have a psychic connection with someone? With who?

Are there any ghost stories near where you live? Tell me some.

Debate: It is possible to use supernatural methods to predict the future

For   Against

Superstition

Do you follow any of these superstitions? Discuss with your partner.

breaking a mirror/spilling salt/stepping on a crack/walking under a ladder/a black cat crossing your path/Friday the thirteenth

Fear

What would scare you the most? Please discuss with a partner.

a haunting/someone who knew the future/someone who could talk to ghosts/someone who could move things with their mind.

Supernatural Happenings

- The Catholic church only accepts one statue of Mary that weeps as legitimate-Our Lady of Akita. The apparition was originally discovered by Sister Agnes Katsuko Sasagawa and lasted from 1973-79.
- 80% of Stigmatics, people who claim to have the wounds of Christ, are women.
- An 'incorruptible' body is different from a mummified one because it has a sweet, or floral scent. It is claimed that many saints have incorruptible bodies.
- Women carried acorns in ancient Britain to look young.
- Turkish people avoid chewing gum at night. It is believed that if you do, you are chewing on the flesh of the dead.
- It was believed that if you met a goat on the way to meeting, that the goat would absorb all of your bad luck.
- In Russia, if a bird poos on you it is good luck.
- The best day to go to a hospital was thought to be Wednesday.
- Also in Russia, if you see a man carrying an empty bucket-it's bad luck. Tsar Alexander II was assassinated by a man carried an empty bucket.
- In France, it is good luck to step in dog pooh with your left foot, but not with your right.

Food

"Nothing is better than going home to family and eating good food and relaxing."

-Irina Shayk

Bread and butter/a lemon/cheap as chips/bring home the bacon/cup of tea/cry over spilled milk/take something with a pinch of salt/bad egg/cheesy

Student A

What are you good at cooking? Why or why not?
What would you like to be better at cooking?
What did you have for breakfast?
What is your favorite food?
What kind(s) of food would you never try?

Student B

What kind of food would you love to try?
What food do you enjoy most from your country or culture?
If you had to eat one food for the rest of your life, what would you eat?
What kind of food is healthy? What kind of food is unhealthy?
What is your favorite comfort food?

Debate: Junk food should be banned or heavily taxed.

<u>For</u>   <u>Against</u>

Perfect Menu

With your partner, prepare a perfect menu for a romantic evening. Choose a starter, a main course, a dessert and a drink.

The Worst Menu

Prepare a menu for someone you hate. With your partner choose a starter, a main course, a dessert and a drink.

Strange Food Facts

- The earliest soup that we have evidence for was a hippopotamus and sparrow meat soup.
- Apples, pears, and plums belong to the plum family.
- The tea bag was invented by accident, the bags were used to send tea samples.
- Castoreum which is used as a flavouring in candies and baked goods, comes from the behinds of beavers.
- Radish and cabbages belong to the same family.
- Mcdonald's sells 75 hamburgers a minute.
- Ketchup was used as a medicine.
- The most expensive fruit in the world is Yubari cantaloupe, one was sold at auction for $23, 500.
- There are 7,500 varieties of apples in the world.
- Carrots used to come in many different colours.

Sports

-Heywood Broun

on the home stretch/front-runner/out of someone's league/par for the course/the ball is in your court/three strikes and you're out/drop the ball/out of left field/hit a home run

Student A

What kind of sports do you play or practice?
What kind of sports would you like to try?
What sports, if any, do you like to watch?
What sports does your country excel in? Which?
Is there any sport that is unique to your country?

Student B

Is there a sport you really hate? Why?
What can a person learn by practicing a sport?
Describe a moment of sport glory in your life.
Describe a moment of sport defeat in your life.
What is a sport that most suits your personality? Why?

Debate: Violent sports should be banned.

For   Against

Role-play…

Choose one famous athlete. Your partner will ask you five questions and you will have to answer as that athlete.

Rules…

With your partner, explain the rules of the following games, *football, volleyball, basketball, hockey, baseball, cricket*

Strange Sports Facts

- If Michael Phelps were a country, he would rank 35th on the all time Olympic gold medal list. He would be ahead of 97 countries.
- When the U.S. beat England in the 1950 World cup, many newspapers thought it was a typo and wrote that England had won 10-1.
- The Philippines have competed in the most Summer Olympics without winning a gold medal.
- During the first modern Olympics, winners were awarded silver medals.
- China did not win an Olympic gold medal until 1984.
- England did not participate in the first three World Cups.
- 60% of NBA players go broke five years after their careers finish.
- The world 'soccer' comes from association football, a name used to distinguish it from Rugby football.
- Ray Caldwell finished pitching a baseball game after being struck by a duck.
- Live pigeon shooting was briefly a part of the Olympic games.

Business

"Making money is an art, and working is an art and good business is the best art."

-Andy Warhol

Ahead of the pack/back to square one/corner the market/easy come, easy go/game plan/my hands are tied/in full swing/keep one's eye on the prize/long shot/no-brainer

Student A

What is the best business to start in your country?
What is the worst business to start in your country?
What is the best business in your neighborhood?
If you could start any business which business would you start?
What is the secret to success in business?

Student B

Think about a business that failed. Why did it fail?
What is the most successful business in your country? How did it become so successful?
Do you think business treat customers fairly in your country? Why or why not?
Have there been any scandals involving businesses in your country? Describe them.
What kind of business have you been involved with in your life?

Debate: The government should do more to encourage local business.

<u>For</u>   <u>Against</u>

The Best Business in the World

With your partner, prepare a short business plan for the best business in the world. Think about your product, or service, your target audience, and a marketing campaign.

The Worst Business in the World

With your partner, prepare a short business plan for the worst business in the world. Think about your product, or service, your target audience, and a marketing campaign.

Strange Business Ideas

Which of these ideas do you think is good? Which would you want to try?

- The Beerbelly sells products that help you hide alcoholic beverages so you can drink in public.
- Potato Parcel writes a message on a potato and delivers it to the person of your choice.
- Cuddle Party hosts hugging parties for lonely people.
- Virtual Dating Assistants does all of the work to get you a date, such as writing your profile. The only thing it doesn't do is go on the date.
- Ugly Furniture makes ugly furniture.
- Dirty Rotten Flowers sends dead and rotting flowers to people you hate.
- Neuticles are artificial implants for pets that have been neutered.
- Reserve a Spot in Heaven allows you to buy your way into Heaven.
- Face Slapping Tata Massage offers to slap your face for money.

Celebrities

-Eddie Vedder.

claim to fame/glamorous/overrated/big name/limelight/star-studded/has-been/household name/big time/infamy/

Student A

Have you met anyone famous? If you have, tell us what happened. If you haven't, tell us who you'd like to meet.
What is the best thing about being a celebrity?
What is the worst thing about being a celebrity?
If you could be famous for one thing, what would it be?
What are you famous for among your friends and family?

Student B

Do you think that celebrities do more good than harm in the world or vice-versa? Why?
What do you think it takes to become a celebrity?
Is there any celebrity who you respect? Why?
Is there any celebrity who you don't like? Why?
You can be a celebrity for one day. Who do you choose and why?

Debate: Celebrities are unhealthy for society

For   Against

Interview

Choose a famous person from your country. Write down five questions you'd like to ask. Your partner has to answer the questions how they think the celebrity would

Schedule

With a partner, choose another famous person and try to decide what their daily routine would look like.

Strange Facts about Celebrities

- Justin Bieber can juggle.
- Johnny Depp is allergic to chocolate.
- Chuck Norris' first name is actually Carlos.
- Robert Downey Jr. (Iron Man, Sherlock Holmes) says Burger King saved him from drug addiction.
- Johnny Depp is also afraid of spiders and clowns.
- Jim Carey wore tap shoes to bed just in case his parents needed cheering up in the middle of the night.
- Morgan Freeman got his private pilot's license at the age of 65.
- Katy Perry had a cat named Kitty Purry.
- Harrison Ford got his break when he was 35 and working as a carpenter. He was noticed by George Lucas, who cast him in Star Wars.
- Steve Jobs became a vegan because he thought it would eliminate the need to bathe.

Cars and driving

-Joseph Gordon Levitt

Car boot sale/car pool/test drive/hit and run/ a way down the road/middle of the road/road hog/panda car/petrol head/gear head

Student A

What do you think is the most dangerous thing about driving in your country?
Have you ever been in a car accident, or other dangerous situation while driving? Please describe.
If you could change any traffic law in your country, what would you change?
What's the most annoying thing about cars? Why?
What's the best thing about cars? Why?

Student B

Are you a good driver? Why or why not? If you don't drive, do you think you would be a good driver? Why or why not?
What kinds of drivers are the best? Why?
What kinds of drivers are the worst?
If you could go for a drive anywhere in the world, where would you go?
Where's the worst place to drive in your town? Why?

Debate: Self-driving cars are a menace to society.

For   Against

Get the motor running...

Think of five places that are great to drive, either in your city, in your country or in your area. Share these with a partner.

Head off for adventure...

Think of five places that you'd love to go for a drive in the world, and think about who you'd like to go with, and what kind of vehicle you'd like to drive. Share these with a partner.

Strange Facts about Cars

- Whale oil was used in some car transmissions until 1973.
- The first electric car was built in 1905.
- The Volkswagen Beetle was originally named the 'Strength Through Joy Car', it was named by Adolf Hitler.
- Mr. H.H. Bliss was the first man to be killed in a car accident in September 1899.
- A Greek taxi driver drove 2.9 million total miles in one a car-a Mercedes.
- The Grapes of Wrath was banned in the Soviet Union after Soviet citizens were amazed that even the poorest of Americans had a car.
- People in Churchill, Canada, leave their car doors open in case a person needs to escape from a polar bear.
- The rearview mirror was invented in 1911.
- Only 139 cars were manufactured for the public in the U.S. during the Second World War from 1941-45.
- In many states, you can be charged with drunk driving if you are sleeping in a car while drunk.

Change

"Change your thoughts and you change your world."

-Norman Vincent Peale

A change for the better/worse/nothing ventured, nothing gained/to be at a crossroads/to blaze a trail/to break new ground/to make headway/to open new doors/to pave the way for something

Student A

What would you like to change about your job?
What would you like to change about your life?
What would you like to change about the world?
What positive change have you made in your life?
What negative change have you made in your life?

Student B

Do you generally have a negative view of change or a positive one? Why?
How have you changed since you were younger?
How will you change in the future?
How has the world changed since you were younger?
What is the biggest change for most people?

Debate: The world is changing too fast.

<u>For</u>   <u>Against</u>

#change

With your partner, discuss five things you'd like to change about your life or personality.

#nochange

With your partner discuss five things you'd never like to change about your life or personality.

The Oldest

- A Eucalyptus tree is around 13,000 years old. It is one of five individuals left in its species.
- There is an underwater meadow of Posidonia seagrass (which is one organism) between Ibiza and Formentera which is 100, 000 years old.
- There is a shrub that is a relative of parsley that lives in the Atacama Desert that can live to be over 2000 years old.
- The Welwistchia is a primitive species of tree with two leaves that lives in Namibia. It can survive for over two thousand years.
- Huon Pine trees in Tasmania have been proven to be over 10, 000 years old.
- A clam named Ming was proven to have lived for over 507 years. It was accidentally killed by scientists studying climate change.
- A goldfish named Hanako lived for 226 years.
- Red sea urchins are believed to be immortal, if they aren't eaten by natural predators.
- Greenland sharks can live up to 400 years old.
- A species of jellyfish is also practically immortal. They revert back to a premature state when they are stressed. They are immortal as long as they aren't eaten.

Charities and helping others

-Miriam Margolyes

To help oneself/charity mugger/vermont charity/charity begins at home/charity case/fundraiser/donation/humanitarian/handout/soup kitchen

Student A

What kinds of charities do a good job in your community?
What kinds of charities do a bad job in your community?
Have you ever given any money to a charity organization? If you have, which one and why? If you haven't, which one would you like to give to?
Have you ever volunteered your time for a worthy cause? Which? If you haven't, which cause would you volunteer for?

Student B

What kind of people do you have the most compassion for?
A *charity mugger* is someone who may be paid by a charity to approach people on the street and ask for donations. What do you think about this strategy?
Vermont charity is quite popular on social media nowadays. How can people be motivated to help others rather than just feel sympathetic?
Do you think it is better to give money or your time?
Have you or someone you know ever needed charity? If you'd like, please describe what happened.

Debate: Everyone has a responsibility to give to charity

For   Against

Perfect

Imagine the perfect charity. With your partner, discuss three things it does right.

Horrible

Imagine the worst charity. With your partner, discuss three things it does wrong.

Strange Charities

Which of these charities do you think is actually a great idea? Why?

- The Critter Connection is an organization that rescues Guinea Pigs and finds them loving homes.
- Helping Hands trains monkeys to help people with disabilities.
- Reuniting Battling Buddies reunites military service dogs with their handlers.
- Tall Clubs International gives scholarships to tall people.
- The 501st Legion are Star Wars fans who have been fundraising for other charities since 1977.
- Child's Play provides games for children to play with when they are in the hospital.
- Naked Clowns raise funds for multiple sclerosis research.
- LongHopes Donkey Shelter helps find good homes for abandoned donkeys.
- The Order of the Azure Rose is dedicated to giving etiquette lessons.
- Heifer International allows you to donate a cow to whoever you choose.

Holidays

" I once wanted to become an atheist, but I gave up- they have no holidays."

-Henry Youngman

All holidays/busman's holiday/hell on a holiday/trim the tree/holiday spirit/be there with bells on/christmas came early/like turkeys voting for an early christmas/the proof is in the pudding/gobble up

Student A

What is your favourite holiday? Why?

What is your least favourite holiday? Why?

Are there any holidays or celebrations that are unique to your country, town or culture? Please describe them.

How are international holidays, like Christmas or Ramadan different in your country?

Is there a holiday that doesn't exist, but you think should?

Student B

What is the most important holiday for you? Why?

What is the least important holiday for you? Why?

Tell us about a special memory you have from a holiday.

What is the strangest holiday or festival you have ever heard of?

What is your favourite/least favourite holiday food?

Debate: Holidays are a waste of time and money

For   Against

Holidays

With your partner come up with five new holidays, either for your country, for your town, or for your family.

Budget Holiday

You have one hundred dollars. You can go on vacation to the next town. What would you do?

Menu

Design the perfect menu, with your partner, for Christmas.

Strangest Holidays

- The Lopburi Monkey Buffet was started as a way to deal with rude monkeys. The monkeys were harassing tourists and asking for food. A festival was started where the monkeys are given a feast of food every year.
- In Bolivia, there is a 'punch your neighbour' festival. The blood is a sacrifice to a local goddess, but it is used as an excuse to beat your neighbours.
- In Spain, there is Antzar Eguna or goose day. Young men try to decapitate a dead goose which is hung in the middle of the town's harbour. No one knows why this started.
- In North America, on February 2nd, a groundhog sees or doesn't see his/her shadow. If the groundhog sees its shadow on Groundhog Day, it will go back into its burrow and there will be six more weeks of winter. If it doesn't see it, winter will finish sooner.
- During the Feast of Anastenaria people celebrate by walking over hot coals. It was originally celebrate to commemorate the burning of a church. People went inside the church to save the icons of Saint Constantine and Saint Helena. It is celebrated in Northern Greece and Southern Bulgaria.
- Hadaka Matsuri Festival-in Japan-it's called the Naked Man festival and it's held on the coldest night of the year. It is held to test the men's bravery.
- Straw Bear Day is held in England in January. A man dresses up as a straw bear and dances in exchange for food and beer.
- La Tomatina is another Spanish Festival with unclear origins. Now it is a yearly tomato fight held annually in Bunol Spain.

Friends

-Mencius

A friend in need is a friend indeed/bosom friends/fast friends/friends in high places/fair weather friends/friends with benefits/false friends/friend zone/friend of Bill W.

Student A

How many friends do you have? Is this too few, too many, or enough?
Tell us about a time when a friend disappointed you.
Tell us about a time when you disappointed a friend.
What do you do when you meet your friends?
How often do you meet your friends?

Student B

Please finish the sentence: A friend is….
Who is your best friend. Why is this person your best friend?
Who is more important in your life, your friends or your family? Why?
Is there anyone who you've never met, but you think you would be friends with?
What's the best way to meet new friends?

Debate: Friends are more important than family

<u>For</u>   <u>Against</u>

Perfect

With your partner, come up with five characteristics of the perfect friend.

The Worst

With your partner, come up with five characteristics of the worst friend.

Strangest Facts about Friendship

- Many animals can make friends with animals that do not belong to their own species. These include chimpanzees, baboons, horses, elephants, dolphins, and of course, humans.
- You make on average 396 friends in your life, but only one in twelve friendships last.
- Not having any friends is as bad for you as smoking or being overweight.
- A marriage based on friendship lasts longer than any other.
- People who have a major illness are more likely to survive if they have a good network of friends.
- Your brain reacts the same way if you are in danger, or a friend is.
- Good friends reduce stress.
- They also influence your weight. If they eat healthy, so will you.
- Our best friends share most of our personal traits.

Environment

-Albert Einstein

A drop in the ocean/a ray of sunshine/voice in the wilderness/answer the call of nature/at sea/beat around the bush/can't see the forest for the trees/down to earth/in deep water/under a cloud/under the weather/neck of the woods

Student A

What is the most beautiful natural environment in your town, in your area, in your country?
What impact have humans had on the environment in your area?
What is your government or community doing to improve the environment?
Tell us about an environmental success story. A time when the situation improved.
What do you think is the most serious environmental problem? Why?

Student B

What do you do to help the environment?
Do you think we will be able to fix the problems with our environment, or is it too late? Why?
What is the most effective way to get people to care about the environment and to change their behaviour?
In what kind of environment do you feel the happiest?
In what ways can what we eat help the environment?

Debate: The government should do more to protect the environment

<u>For</u>   <u>Against</u>

The Worst...

Which of these Environmental problems is the worst?

overpopulation/climate change/extinction/clean water, air/over fishing, deforestation/

With your partner, choose one of the above issues, and come up with five ways to solve the problem.

Shocking Facts about the Environment

- The amount of water on earth is constant, which means the water molecules you drink every day were also drunk by dinosaurs.
- 40% of all bottled water sold on earth is bottled tap water.
- 27, 000 trees are cut down each day to make toilet paper.
- Paper can only be recycled six times. After that the fiber is too weak.
- Pollution has killed more than 100 million people worldwide.
- Aluminum can be recycled again and again.
- 137 species a day go extinct in tropical forests.
- Humans are responsible for the extinction of 1 million species.
- Plastic kills 1 million marine animals a year.
- Only 1% of people who live in Chinese cities have clean air.

City Life

"The city is not a concrete jungle, it is a human zoo."

-Desmond Morris

Can't fight city hall/cardboard city/city slicker/fat city/barf city/cement city/

Student A

What is the best thing about living in a city?
What is the worst thing about living in a city?
How would you improve your city? Why do you want this to happen?
How has your city or town changed since you were a child?
Would you prefer to live in the city or in the country?

Student B

If you could live in any city in the world, where would you live?
What's the most interesting city to visit in your country?
What do you worry about if you live in a city?
What areas of your city are safe?
What areas are dangerous?

Debate: Which is better, life in the city or life in the country?

City Life		Country Life	
Pro	Con	Pro	Con

Mayor: You, with your partner have been selected as mayor of your city, how would you solve these problems?

Homelessness
Too much traffic
Pollution/garbage
Recreation for families, for teenagers, for the elderly, etc

Compare: How is your city better and worse than the following cities?

Dubai   New York   London   Berlin   Tokyo   Moscow

Strange City Facts

- You can buy espresso at 181 places in Paris.
- 29% of pollution in San Francisco comes from China.
- The oldest synagogue in the world is located in Cairo-the Ben Ezra Synagogue.
- There are more bridges in Berlin than there are in Venice.
- Also in Berlin, 125 tonnes of sausages are consumed daily.
- Honking your horn in traffic in New York is illegal.
- New York was the first capital of the United States.
- New Yorkers bite 10 times more people per year than sharks do.
- New York has the second largest Polish population in the world-after Warsaw.
- It also has the largest Jewish population outside of Israel.

Complaining

-Zig Ziglar

Can't complain/nothing to complain about/complain of/complain to/leave a lot to be desired/hard to please/crabby/grumble/worry

Student A

What kind of things do you complain the most about?
Why do you think people complain about you?
Does complaining make you feel better or better worse?
When was the last time you complained about something?
When was the last time someone complained to you?

Student B

Have you ever had to complain at a restaurant or a shop? What happened?
What kind of people do you think complain more?
What kind of things do people complain about the most?
How often do you complain? Do you think this is a lot or a little?
Do you think men and women complain about the same things or different things? Why?

Debate: Men complain more than women

<u>For</u>   <u>Against</u>

Role-play

You have bought a defective item from a shop. Your partner works at the shop. Have a conversation where you want to get your money back. When you've finished, switch roles.

Mr./Miss/Mrs. President

The president of your country suddenly appears. Complain about five things.

Complaints from the Mayfair

Here are a list of complaints that were submitted to different hotel. What do you think of them?

- The sheets are too white
- The sea was too blue
- Ice cream too cold
- Bath was too big
- Girlfriend's snoring kept guest awake (discount requested)
- Guest's dog didn't enjoy his stay (refund requested)
- Hotel had no ocean view (in Mayfair, London and Italy, 80km from coast)
- There was no steak on vegetarian menu
- Waiter was too handsome
- Mother of Groom wasn't given the honeymoon suite

Travelling

Miss the boat/in the same boat/rock the boat/put the cart before the horse/drive up the wall/back street driver/my way or the highway/hit the road/on the home stretch

Student A

Where was the last place you traveled to?
If you could travel anywhere in the world, where would you travel to?
Where would you never want to travel?
Where is the best place in your country to travel?
Who is the worst person you know to travel with?

Student B

What is the worst thing that happened to you when you were on a trip?
What is the best thing that happened to you when you were on a trip?
What's has been your most interesting trip?
Why do you travel?
What do you like to do when you are on vacation?

Debate: Travel to national parks should be banned.

<u>For</u>   <u>Against</u>

Road Trip

You have one hundred dollars plan a trip around your country. You have to stop at least four places.

World Trip

You have one thousand dollars to plan a trip around the world. You have to stop at least four places.

Strangest Facts about Travelling in the US

- Portion sizes about 80% bigger than they are in Europe.
- There are drive-ins everywhere. There are drive-in liquor stores, and even drive-in daiquiri stores.
- Ads for lawyers and legal services are everywhere.
- There are also ads for prescription medicine everywhere.
- The squirrels are apparently terrifying.
- The houses, and the spaces between houses are huge.
- The cars are massive.
- Americans smile too much.
- The price on products in stores in the US. doesn't include tax.

Think of a foreign country you have visited. What surprised you?

Current Events

-Victoria Justice

Wise after the event/blessed event/in the event of/to make an event/turn of events/bearer of bad news/make news/fake news/break the news

Student A

What is currently going on in your country?
What is currently going on in your town?
What is currently going on in your family?
What is going on in your life?
What do you wish were happening in all of these areas now?

Student B

What area of current events do you follow the most closely-i.e. Politics, sports, etc.
What area of current events do you wish you knew more about? Why?
Why is the news on television, or on the internet so depressing?
Can you think of some happy news you recently have heard?
What news are you most looking forward to?

Debate: The media is responsible for how we view the world

For   Against

Stranger Things

Tell your partner the five strangest things that have ever happened to you and explain, why, in your opinion these things happened to you.

Very Current News

Tell your partner five things that are going on in your life today.

Strangest Scandals

- In 1919, the Navy town of Newport, Rhode Island was rumored to have a thriving gay scene. In order to 'out' people who were gay, the Navy paid young, attractive men to have sex with them.
- Bob Packwood denied harassing women. He was a prominent US Congressman. It turned out that he had kept a diary for thirty years where he described in graphic detail what he did.
- Douglas R. Stringfellow claimed to be a WWII veteran who had lost the use of his legs due to being tortured by the Gestapo. He was elected to Congress. Shortly later, it was discovered that he made the whole story up and could walk.
- Robert Jonson, vice President to Martin Van Buren, once owned his wife. She was his father's former slave, they fell in love and the law said that they couldn't get married.

Dating and Relationships

"There are only two people in your life you should lie to...the police and your girlfriend

-Jack Nicholson

ask somebody out/chat somebody up/go out with someone/hit on someone/hook up with someone/lead someone on/make out with someone/to stand someone up/to turn down someone

Student A

How old were you when you went on your first date? Do you think this was too young, or old or just right?

Who was the last person you asked out on a date?

Who should ask someone out, the man or the woman, or does it matter?

What is something you should never do on a date?

What is something you should always do on a date?

Student B

Do you think it's okay to date more than one person at a time? Why or why not?

If you were single, and you could ask anyone out on a date, who would you ask?

Would you ever consider dating someone from a different religion or culture?

What is the best date you have ever been on?

What is the worst date you have ever been on?

Debate: Parents should choose who their children date

<u>For</u>   <u>Against</u>

Perfect Date

Try to imagine the perfect date for you and your partner (in class) you both have to decide on something that you would like to go.

Dating Catastrophe

Imagine all the things that could go wrong on a date. Discuss them with your partner.

Strange Dating Sites

- AgeMatch.com for men who are looking for much younger women.
- TallFriends.com for really tall people who are looking for love.
- WealthyMen.com for ladies who are really focussed on marrying well.
- GlutenfreeSingles. For people who don't eat gluten.
- Women Behind Bars. For men with really low standards. Or a really high level of desperation.
- Furrymate. For people who like to dress up as animals. Furry ones.
- Sea Captain Date. For sailors.
- Marry Me already. For people who are very impatient.
- Farmers Only. Yes, that's the name. It's only for farmers.
- beautifulpeople.com. You have to pass a test. That's how they know you aren't lying.

Crime

"Behind every crime is a story of sadness."

-Enrique Pena Nieto

It's no crime/if you can't do the time, don't do the crime/crime doesn't pay/partner in crime/a steal/beat the rap/hand in the till/on the run/on the dock

Student A

Have you ever witnessed a crime? If you have, what happened?
Have you ever been the victim of a crime? If you have, what happened?
Have you ever committed a crime? If so, what happened?
What is the most common kind of crime in your country/community?
Have you ever had any interaction with the police? What happened?

Student B

What do you think is the worst crime a person can commit?
What can be done to reduce the amount of crime in your community?
Do you think a person who commits a crime can ever return to normal life? Why or why not?
What's the best way to punish criminals?
Why do you think films and books about crime are so popular?

Debate: Capital punishment is the best way to reduce violent crime

For   Against

Perfect Crime

With your partner, try to think about the perfect crime. What would you steal? What kind of planning would you have to do?

The Worst Crime

With your partner, try to think of five things that could go wrong if you really turned to a life in crime.

Strange Crime Facts

- In Paris, in 1926, the Ukrainian Head of State was shot five times. The police walked up the assassin and asked if that was enough.
- The US crime rate is lower than that of the UK.
- A Dutch crime writer wrote a book about a writer who killed his wife. His wife disappeared and he became famous. When the body was discovered, he was charged with murder.
- Isaac Newton fought counterfeiters as an undercover investigator.
- Organized crime is the third largest business in the world.
- The Vatican has the world's highest crime rate.
- Leaving the U.S. with more than $5 in pennies is a crime. The punishment is up to five years in prison.
- Pinball used to be illegal in the US.

Education

---

bookworm/copycat/hit the books/pass with flying colors/skip class/put your thinking cap on/draw a blank/eager beaver

Student A

What was the best thing about your education?
What was the worst thing about your education?
What do you think is the purpose of education? For example, to get a good job, to learn about the world, etc.…
What is something you wish you had learned or wish you had learned better when you were younger?
What is the next thing you'd like to learn?

Student B

Who is the most educated person you know and what makes them so educated?
If you could change the education system in your country, what would you change?
Who was/is the best teacher you had/have and what made/makes them so good?
Who was/is the worst teacher you had/have and what made/makes them so bad?
Do you think you could be a teacher, why or why not?

Debate: People should pay for education

<u>For</u>   <u>Against</u>

Ideal School

If you could design your own school, what courses would you include, and what would you eliminate?

The Worst School

Invent the worst possible school you can imagine. Think of five things that make it so bad.

Strange Facts about Education

- 12% of the world's adult population is illiterate.
- 90% of highs school dropouts in the US are on welfare.
- 2/3rds of illiterate people in the world are women.
- Illiteracy has been linked to high infant death rates, the spread of HIV/AIDS and extreme poverty.
- 70% of children in South Sudan from the age of 6-17 have never been educated.
- 1 in 4 children in the US grow up without learning how to read.
- the oldest university is usually considered to be Nalanda University in India, founded in the 5th century A.D.
- In the United States, 14% of new teachers resign by the end of their first year, 33% leave within their first 3 years, and almost 50% leave by their 5th year.
- Children who are born to educated mothers are less likely to be malnourished or stunted. Each additional year of maternal education decreases the child mortality rate by 2%.
- The countries in the world that have the most people with a tertiary degree include 1) Russian Federation, 2) Canada, 3) Japan, 4) Israel, 5) United States, 6) Korea, 7) Australia, 8) United Kingdom, 9) New Zealand, and 10) Ireland.

Facebook and Social Media

"Social media has colonized what was once a sacred space occupied by emptiness; the space reserved for thought and creativity."

-Mahershala Ali

app/crowdfunding/crowdsourcing/meme/trending/troll/viral/avatar/chat/clickbait

Student A

What kind of social media accounts do you have?
Do you think that social media is generally a good invention or not? Why?
What kind of things do you post on social media, if you do post anything? If you don't, why not?
What is the most annoying behavior on social media?
What is the best social network site?

Student B

What kind of features do you think social networking sites should have?
Have you ever 'lurked' on social media sites? 'Lurking' means to look for your former girlfriends, boyfriends, and see what they are doing…
Have you ever had an online relationship? What happened?
In what ways has social media changed people's behavior?

Debate: Social media has changed the world

<u>For</u>   <u>Against</u>

Pros and Cons

With your partner talk about the pros and cons of the following sites: Facebook, Twitter, YouTube, Instagram

Cure the Addict

Your friend is addicted to social media. With your partner, come up with a way to make them less addicted.

Strange Facts about Facebook

- Hackers attempt to break into 600 000 Facebook accounts every day.
- You can change your language on Facebook to 'pirate'.
- The average US user of the sites spends 40 minutes a day on it.
- Al Pacino was the first 'face' on Facebook.
- Smartphone users check Facebook 14 times a day.
- Several people have been murdered for 'unfriending' someone on Facebook.
- There are on average 3.74 degrees of separation between any two people on Facebook.
- Facebook tracks the sites you visit, even after you have signed out.
- 1 in 3 people feel more dissatisfied with their life after visiting Facebook.
- Facebook is primarily blue because Mark Zuckerberg is color-blind.
- There are about 30 million people who have died who still have Facebook accounts.
- In 2011, a third of all divorces in the US involved Facebook in some way.

Entertainment

We aren't in an information age, we are in an entertainment age."

-Tony Robbins

Class clown/to make a clown of yourself/showstopper/ a dog and pony show/run the show/steal the show/party animal/extravaganza/amusement

Student A

What do you do to entertain yourself?
How has entertainment changed since you were little?
How would your entertainment change if you had more money?
If you could be an actor, a singer, or a dancer, which would you choose and why?
How much money do you spend on entertainment per month?

Student B

Is there anything that other people find exciting that bores you?
Is there anything that bores other people yet excites you?
What would be your idea of a perfect birthday party?
What's something fun that you've never tried, and yet would love to?
How much time do you spend everyday doing things you enjoy? Do you think this is too little, too much or just enough?

Debate: People spend too much time and money on entertainment

<u>For</u>   <u>Against</u>

Are you not entertained?

Your partner is bored. Suggest five things you could do together to have a great time.

Are you not entertained (budget edition)?

You meet your partner again, but this time they have no money. Suggest five things you could do for fun in your town with no money.

Strange Entertainment Facts

- O.J. Simpson, famous celebrity murderer, was turned down for the part of the Terminator, because he looked too nice.
- 'Psycho' was released in black and white because its director, Alfred Hitchcock thought it would be too graphic in color.
- Barack Obama got to watch 'Game of Thrones' episodes before anyone else when he was president.
- Mickey Mouse has a sister named Amelia Fieldmouse.
- The series 'Dexter' inspired three real life killings.
- Malaysia banned screenings of 'Fifty Shades of Grey'. France, however, permit people as young as twelve to watch the film.
- The chills you get when you listen to music are called 'musical frisson'.
- The longest movie ever made lasts 85 hours and is called, 'The Cure for Insomnia'.
- Walt Disney World is the U.S's second largest buyer of explosives, after the Department of Defense.

Controversial Topics

-Judith Martin

Bone of contention/bone to pick/difference of opinion/war of words/contentious/conflicted/disapproval/groupthink/spar/squabble

Student A

What's an unpopular opinion you have?
Is there something that everyone believes now that you think few people in the future will believe?
If yes, what is it?
What are the most controversial topics in your country?
What are the most controversial topics in your town or community?
What are the most controversial topics in your family?

Student B

Are there any controversial topics that the media focuses too much on in your country? Which?
Is there something that you think people should care about, and yet they don't? What is it?
Who is the person you argue with the most? Why do you think it is that person?
Why do you think controversial topics are controversial?
What has been the biggest controversy of your life?
Write down five controversial topics. Share your opinion with the class.

Debate: As a class choose a current controversial issue. Divide into two groups to debate it.

Couple Fight

Here are some of the most common things couples fight about, tell your partner if you fight about these things or if you would: *text messages/politics/sharing too much on social media/spending too much time on the phone/room temperature/sex*

Stupid Arguments

Here are some of the most stupid arguments ever, with your partner discuss if you have ever argued about some of these things: *toilet paper, over or under/peeing, sitting or standing/people being angry to you in a dream/do green flowers exist/when does the afternoon start/*

Your stupid arguments…

Tell your partner some of the stupid things you've argued about.

Discrimination

"Let's practice motivation and love, not discrimination and hate."

-Zendaya

Discriminate against/discriminate between/intolerance/ableism/ageism/nepotism/differentiate/sexual discrimination/racial discrimination

Student A

What kind of discrimination is most common in your country? Why do you think this is so?
What kind of discrimination have you faced in your life?
Why do you think people discriminate against others?
What can be done to reduce the amount of discrimination?
What do you think is the worst kind of discrimination?

Student B

Are people from your country or community discriminated against in any way? How?
Do you think discrimination is ever necessary? When?
Are people becoming more tolerant, or less tolerant?
Do you think animals can be discriminated against? How?
If you have never been discriminated against, how would you react if someone did discriminate against you?

Debate: Discrimination is natural

   For   Against

A person of fine discrimination

A person of fine discrimination means someone who has excellent taste. With your partner, discuss which of these you are a person of discrimination and in which you have horrible taste: books, film, food, the opposite sex

To differentiate...

To be able to differentiate means to be able to tell the difference between two things. With your partner, say how many colors you can distinguish in this room.

Unusual discriminations

Here are some strange things people are discriminated for having. Have you ever been discriminated against because of these things?

being a bald man/being a ginger/being overweight/having a speech impediment/being ugly/having a strange name/your accent/how old you are/how short you are

Family

-Michael J. Fox

Family man/black sheep/to run in the family/in the family way/flesh and blood/relative/relation/next of kin/folks/mum's the word

Student A

Who is your favourite member of your family? Why?

How much quality time do you spend with your family? When was the last time you did so?

Which is better, to have a big family or a small family? Why?

If you could change one thing about your family, what would you change?

What is the secret to having a happy family life?

Student B

Which prepares you better for life, a family full of happiness and little conflict, or a family full of conflict and struggle?

Who or what should a person be more loyal to: family, friends, country, religion?

How have you helped out your family? How have they helped out you?

You discover that you are adopted. Does this change how you feel about your family? Why or Why not?

Are pets real members of the family, or are they just pets?

Debate

Parents should stay together for the children

Pro   Con

Ideal Family

Tell your partner what your ideal family would look like. How members does it have, what do they do, how do they interact, where do they live.

Real Family

Tell your partner about your real family, about all of its members, what are the relationships between people like, who's the black sheep of the family, etc.

Weird Family Law

- In France, it is legal to marry a dead person. Instead of saying I do, you say I did.
- In Montana, you don't need to go to your own wedding. You can appoint someone as a proxy instead.
- In Kentucky, it is illegal to marry someone more than four times.
- In Dubai, you need to pass a doctor's examination before you get married.
- In Delaware, you can annul a marriage if you got married on a dare.
- In New York, you can sue someone who you think caused the failure of your marriage (apart from your spouse)
- In the Phillipines, adults under the age of 25 must get their parents' advice before getting married.
- Also in the Philippines, a widow has to wait 301 days after her husband died to get remarried.
- Finally, in the Philippines it is legal to murder your spouse or another person if you catch them cheating.

The Future

> "The future belongs to those who believe in the beauty of their dreams."

-Eleanor Roosevelt

Any minute now/the future looks bright/in the near future/right around the corner/sign of things to come/bound to happen/time will tell/to get ahead of yourself/like there's no tomorrow/in the offing/close at hand

Student A

What do you think will happen in your future?
What do you think will happen in the future of your country?
What do you think will happen in the future of the world?
Do believe it is possible to predict the future using cards, crystal balls, etc. Why or why not?
How do you think the future will surprise you?

Student B

How is your present different from the future you imagined for yourself when you were younger?
Who do you think has the brightest future of the people you know?
Which businesses and industries have the brightest future?
Which businesses and industries have the dimmest future?
If you could have complete control of your future, what would it look like?

Debate:

The Future will be better:

For   Against

Better/worse...

your life/your town/your city/the world/your family....How will these places and things be better and worse ten years in the future.

Future person

A person from one thousand years in the future travels to our time. Think of five questions you'd like to ask. Your partner has to think of what they would say.

Wrong Predictions

- Albert Einstein predicted in 1932 that nuclear energy would be impossible.
- Decca records declined to sign the Beatles, one of the most profitable music groups in history, in 1962, because Decca believed guitar music was a fad.
- Western Union said that the telephone would never be successful in 1876.
- Ronald Reagan, former US president was once rejected for a role as a president because he didn't look presidential enough.
- Dr. Dionysius Lardner wrote in 1830 that rail travel would be impossible at high speeds because people would be unable to breathe.
- Lord Kelvin in 1883 wrote that x-rays would be proven to be a hoax.
- A Michigan bank refused to invest in Henry Ford's new company in 1903, because automobiles were a 'novelty'.
- In 1954, the National Cancer Institute claimed that smoking did not cause lung cancer.
- IBM told the founders of Xerox that photocopiers had no future.

Gambling

-Wilson Mizner

Ace in the hole/ace in the sleeve/go for broke/all bets are off/hit the jackpot/hedge your bets/a long shot/ante up/bet the farm/no dice

Student A

What kind of gambles do you make in your daily life?
What is the biggest gamble you have made in your life?
What kind of gambling is legal in your country?
Do you think there are any moral problems with gambling? Why or why not?
Do you know anyone who had a problem with gambling? How did they get help?

Student B

What is a bigger gamble- love or business?
Have you ever tried to gamble? If you have, what did you gamble on?
What would you do if you won the lottery?
Have you ever been to a casino? If yes, please describe your experiences.
What is the most addictive kind of gambling? Why do you think so?

Debate: Gambling should be completely legal

For   Against

Role Play

Imagine you meet someone who has a problem with gambling. Think of five questions you'd ask. Your partner has to answer what they think the addict would say.

Casino

You have five hundred dollars to spend in a casino. What would you do? Discuss with your partner?

Strange Facts about Gambling

- Citizens of Monaco can't gamble in casinos in Monaco.
- Casinos in Las Vegas organized tours of atomic testing in the early 1950s.
- Card counting in Blackjack is not illegal, but it is frowned upon.
- The sandwich takes its name from the Earl of Sandwich. Legend has it that he was so busy gambling that he didn't want to stop to eat lunch, and he asked for a slice of meat between two pieces of bread.
- The first slot machine was invented by a mechanic as a game to entertain people who were waiting for him to finish.
- Casinos are illegal in Japan, but Pachinko parlors are not. You play a game, and win a steel ball that you can exchange in government operated offices for money.
- You can gamble, bet on sports in Las Vegas, but you can not buy a lottery ticket.
- Macau, the only city in China where it is legal to gamble, is much more profitable than Las Vegas.
- The roulette wheel is called the Devil's wheel-the numbers add up to 666.